T0129443

THROUGH
A
BLACK MAN'S
EYES

KEVIN L. ALEEM

WITH COVER AND CHAPTER
ILLUSTRATIONS BY
VANNETTA WOOD

Order this book online at www.trafford.com
or email orders@trafford.com

Most Trafford titles are also available at major online book retailers.

Print information available on the last page.

ISBN: 978-1-4120-0525-8 (sc)

Trafford rev. 10/18/2019

 www.trafford.com
North America & international
toll-free: 1 888 232 4444 (USA & Canada)
fax: 812 355 4082

DEDICATION

MOTHER AFRICA MAY BE THE ROOT AND LIFE
GIVING SOIL OF THE
AFRICAN AMERICAN.
HOWEVER,
GOD CHOSE TO PLANT MY ROOTS IN A DIFFERENT
SOIL.
THEREFORE,
I DEDICATE THIS WORK TO MY LIFE GIVING SOIL
AND MAN MOLDER,
MY MOTHER JOLENE TYSON.

"Many a black man has gotten the inspiration of his career from Poetry.............and when they start to think poetic they realize that after all life is not only an empty dream."

MARCUS GARVEY
(NEW JAMAICAN, 26 JANUARY 1933)

FORWARD

The question of what is in the heart and soul of black men is often pondered in our places of worship, in our homes, on our street corners, and even in academic settings specifically designed for, or targeted to blacks. Ralph Ellison touched on it in <u>The Invisible Man</u>, as did Richard Wright in <u>Native Son</u>. This work attempts to address this often ignored, yet frequently discussed topic as it relates to African American males socially, economically, psychologically and intimately.

For some time now, I've had the privilege of reading Kevin Aleem's work of both poetry and prose. With each reading, even today, every piece leaves me feeling something a little different. What's remarkable about it is that sometimes, once you've finished a particular piece, you have to put it down and think, really think. You are not quite sure what to feel because he's expressed a thought on a topic in a way that you might not have experienced before. A piece may speak to you in such a way as to bring a smile of familiarity across your face. Other pieces may render you speechless, shaking your head or sucking your teeth with disbelief or in disagreement, or to cause a nod of your head in concurrence.

Sounds simplistic, but the ability to create something that touches you deep within, really is not. It doesn't always matter what it touches, a dangerous notion for some individuals with twisted propensities, but generally speaking, it doesn't matter: the soul, a raw nerve, a *good or bad* memory. The ability to do that, to create that which touches, moves or stirs something inside of someone you've never met and may never meet, is a gift for the reader, and an indescribable gift for the writer. How the reader feels upon completing a writer's work versus the way a writer feels upon finishing the work is dichotomous, at best. The reader may or may not like what they've read, and likewise for the writer. (Generally, if the writer does not like what he's written, it doesn't see the light of day!) However, the occasion when the feelings of the reader and writer reach congruency is when the writer and the reader are moved in the same way by what has been created.

Well, you may not get that exact sense of congruency here. Kevin's not the kind of writer that writes for anyone other than himself. He writes what he feels at the time that he feels it. It's not quite the same type of arrogance that most seasoned writers warn novice writers about either. Its honesty and confidence: the message sent is genuine, real and true; and the writer respects the reader's ability to get the message. Don't be put off by the prospect of not getting the message, because what you'll find is that the use of language in most instances is so interesting, you'll be compelled to give it a second read out of sheer curiosity, if not surprise, and not for comprehension.

Don't feel too manipulated either, because it's no coincidence that you'll find yourself giving different pieces a second (*or even a third*) read.

Artful? Yes. Deliberate? Absolutely, his intention is to have you question what he means.

From one writer to another, may your message be received by all those who can identify with the African American male experience in all its glory, splendor, diversity, pain and richness, and all those who care to understand that experience. From one reader to another, may you enjoy the birth of this man's familiar, yet refreshing new work.

DONNA ECHOLS-KEARSE
AUTHOR
MEMBER of the AFRICAN AMERICAN
WOMEN WRITERS GROUP, ISSA
PHILADELPHIA, PA.

EYES ON CONTENTS

THOUGHTS

LOVE AND LIFE

MORE THOUGHTS

EYES
ON THOUGHTS

MY BROTHERS

Though we may appear grown
All secure, smooth and suave
Not all is as it seems
For our heritage we can't solve

For you see we were born as brothers
And it is time to remind each of you
That right will always be right
Yet right won't always be true

For you see injustice is prevalent
All over the place
It doesn't need a reason
Just a color or a race

So we must speak to our rich brothers
Looking at our poor brothers pushed to the side
Tell them to
Use your wealth, knowledge, and power
Reinstall the faith, rebuild the pride

So we must speak to our poor brothers
Angry and taking what isn't yours
Tell them to
Guide themselves in the path of their brothers' progress
Make a dream only they can forge

Remember early on
About how suave we appeared to be?
Well as long as we have well-cooked skin
our spirit is all that is free

For men with color in life
Are ruled by stereotypes in this world
They may be allowed to climb the mountain
Then near the top
Tripped, pushed, or even hurled

Crashing down again
Into life's harsh realities
Trying to make it day by day
Not to be another fatality

Now don't take me wrong
We're not down about our place in life
We're just getting a little sick and tired
Of the struggle, fuss, and fight

Please my brothers' think
Because thinking is a must
We must be careful in this life
Careful whom we trust

So you see my beloved brothers
There is no need to fight from within
We've got enough external problems
It's time to unite
It's time to look to God
It's time to be brothers once again

WHEN

When does inspiration
Become the catalyst for motivation

When does motivation
Become the drive for thought

When does thought
Become the sweat of labor

When does labor
Become the outlook for completion

When does completion
Become the warmth of a good feeling

When does that good feeling
Become a love of what you are doing

When does what you are doing
Become internally fulfilling

When does being fulfilled
Become what is really needed

When does what is needed
Become the strive for when

When, Black Man, does when
Become **Now**

I CAN TOUCH

I can touch one person to share my knowledge
Infinite of Infantile
No matter the mental condition, physical condition,
or normalcy
I CAN TOUCH one person

I can touch the multitudes to share my opinion
Whether it's Liked or Disliked
No matter the diversity of the crowd, its color creed
or race
I CAN TOUCH the multitudes

I can touch the rich to share my words
From the Poor
No matter whether it falls on deaf ears, is ignored
or accepted
I CAN TOUCH the rich

I can touch the poor to share my empathy for
Their Struggle to Succeed
No matter how broken the heart is due to failed
or crushed attempts
I CAN TOUCH the poor

I can touch the disabled to share my help
All I Can Give
No matter whether it is viewed as sympathy
or accepted freely
I CAN TOUCH the disabled

I can touch you to share this important point
Whether you Agree or Disagree
No matter how strongly you agree
or disagree

I CAN TOUCH you
For the point is
You have been touched
Because **you** are the

I

I HAD A TALK TODAY

I had a talk with God today
I prayed to the Creator and made a request
I worshipped and requested wisdom
The wisdom of self-respect, appreciation, and choice
And like a warm blanket of love I received my answer
Stating listen to those who are most dear to you

&

The world's love will fall upon your heart

So I had a talk with my mother, a black woman,
The Queen

&

The Queen told me
For law and order, never trust a black lawyer
For a white lawyer is more competent
And will provide you with your best chances
In this racist world and
Her words fell with a family's love upon my ears

So I had a talk with my father, a black man,
The King
&
The King told me
For business, always follow the lead of the white man
For a white man has the business knowledge
And the connections you need
In this racist world and
His words fell with a family's love upon my ears

So I had a talk with my brother, a warrior,
The Prince
&

The Prince told me

To get ahead in life, always have a hustle

For if you have a hustle you have a way to survive

Because the white man will only allow you so much success

In this racist world and

His words fell with a family's love upon my ears

So I had a talk with my sister, a scribe,
The Princess
&
The Princess told me

When in trouble, fear the black man and search out the white

For black men are cowardly and shiftless

And white men exude pride

In this racist world and

Her words fell with a family's love upon my ears

So I had a talk with my child, a black child
The Innocent Vision of My Future
&
The Vision told me

I, The Black Child, Will be the best at whatever I attempt!

I, The Black Child, Will challenge the stereotypes!

I, The Black Child, Will succeed!

I, The Black Child, Will re-create this racist world!

&

The child's words fell with the worlds love upon my

HEART!

For, Thank God, it was the child that I **listened** to!!!

SIT DOWN SHUT UP AND LISTEN

Mother, Father, Family, Mentors, and, Friends.
I now understand why, and how you tried to mold me
through my developmental years
With the words,
" Sit down, Shut up, Listen, and you'll be all right."

I understand that it was not my time to speak,
to challenge, to change,
Because I was learning about discipline,
how to speak, how to challenge, and what to change.

Yet, now I don't understand.
For I am a man, a proud black man,
yet your advice in facing this racist world is
STILL,
Sit down, Shut up, Listen, and you'll be all right.
Yet, as this man did not remain a boy,
The same rule doesn't always apply.
Thus the way it was,
may not be the way it is,
And may be grossly inadequate
for the way it needs to be.

I can no longer just sit down,
For a man who refuses to take a stand,
is destined for submissive servitude
and submissive servitude is too close to slavery for me.

9

I as a man who takes a stand,
can now make a choice.
A choice of
who I am, what I am, and what I shall be.
Thus strengthening the pride of my stand.

I can no longer shut up,
For injustice, racism, and prejudice
must be approached, dissuaded, and addressed,
because these evils draw strength in my silence,
And their covert existence breeds an overt pattern
of that's the way it was and
that's the way it ought to be.

I look at the recognized heroes of my race,
Malcolm, Martin, Marcus, Mandela,
and say to myself,
" What if they and all the other recognized and unrecognized
heroes had just shut up,
without speaking up and challenging?"

I can no longer just listen without responding,
For silence is deadly and
ignorance is far from bliss.
For as I remain silent and portray ignorance,
I continue to endure the beatings offered
with all the stinging pain of an overseer's whip.

I have listened to learn and
learned to make a difference.
A difference undone by the power of silence.

Therefore, I will continue to listen and learn
for the purpose of completing the circle of knowledge
with my response, my opinion, my thoughts.
Thus destroying the myth of my ignorance,
and the misperception of my concurrence,
interpreted in my silence.

Yes, I will be all right!
Please don't fear for my safety
For the strength of my ancestors
and the shield of GOD is with me at all times,
as is the guidance and strengths of the recognized heroes,
and heroes that mean even more in my life.
Those being
my mother, my father, my family, my mentors, and my friends.
All of you are a key component of me and my development.

Yes,
to sit down, to shut up, listen,
and let it be all right
would be easy.
It also would not be what you raised me to be,
A BLACK MAN, A LEADER, A KING.

TO WONDER

HAVE YOU EVER WONDERED
How wonderful it is to wonder

HAVE YOU EVER WONDERED
How love
The world's oldest and most needed emotion
Is also the most destructive

HAVE YOU EVER WONDERED
What it feels like to hurt, yet, you cannot place the pain

HAVE YOU EVER WONDERED
How it feels to need, yet not be needed

HAVE YOU EVER WONDERED
How it feels to want, yet not be wanted

HAVE YOU EVER WONDERED
What makes you lonely in an overcrowded world

HAVE YOU EVER WONDERED
What makes us give our hearts
Whether it's for the good or the bad

HAVE YOU EVER WONDERED
How greatness feels when left unshared

HAVE YOU EVER WONDERED
How beautiful you are or how beautiful you shall become

I believe the time has come to wonder
Because to wonder is to feel
As to feel is the key of life

WONDERFUL LIFE !

TOUCHED BY DRUGS

The smile of a modern day pusher.
The joy of his Benz, Bling, and fame
Is the true look of
The doctor of death

The shakes of the tormented child
The expression of a mind stymied and unfulfilled
Is the true look of
The drug-touched future

The tears of the mother
The closing of the casket
Is the true look of
The drug-stung family

The pain of the bullet riddled body
The feeling of life as it leaves
Is the true look of
A Blackman who could not pay

The shameless waste of emotions
The awesome waste of life
Is the true look of
Those, whose lives are touched by drugs

HERITAGE

Why do I fight against my own heritage?
This question burns so very deep yet, when I stop and think
The answer flows so very clear

I yell that I am oppressed
Then I turn and do more damage to my people and myself
Than any other man, race, or creed could ever do

I belittle my women
I drug my mind
I steal from my mother
I call my friend slave
I abuse my child
I kill my brother,
yet
I yell that I am oppressed

The time has come for me
The time to learn
The time to think
The time to stop the abuse
Of myself and my people,
yet
I yell that I am oppressed

I as one part of a black nation
Must learn how to not fight from within
I must learn to
Join our strength
Join our joy
Join our talent
Join our fame,
yet
I yell that I am oppressed

I have power and I have pride
Which flows from the strengths of my people
The multitudes of tears from mothers, for the sons lost,
yet
I yell that I am oppressed

The only true answer to my oppression
Is to remove the self-imposed oppression first
To look for the peace and strength within

To let the dream never die
To start with the one and only

I

EYES
ON LOVE AND LIFE

A BLACK MAN'S LOVE

A BLACK MAN'S LOVE

It is true
A true and deep feeling love
A love so deep
That it makes him feel
The pain of passion and
The joy of jealousy

A BLACK MAN'S LOVE

It doesn't always show
Yet when nurtured and treated right
It comes out from deep in the heart
A heart hardened, yet compassionate and
Is shown in the strength of his eyes
As bright and as fiery as the sun itself

A BLACK MAN'S LOVE

A woman's fantasy and quest
Something they want and desire
Yet feel that it can never be
A love lost in insecurities

A BLACK MAN'S LOVE

Once it is caught and exposed
It cannot and will not be caged
It must continue to be free
And to be nurtured
To fly as a dove
To grow and maintain the strength of only

A BLACK MAN'S LOVE

PASSION

Hello! My name is passion
Or is it Drive, Desire, or Lustt
Confusion clouds my thoughts
Though my focus for you is a must

For you see I may try
To avoid struggle and stray
Yet, I could never leave you for long
Because my heart will be longing to stay

It may hurt deep inside
Yet, this pain is really a joy
It has weakened this lion of a man
Into nothing but a puppy of a boy

Confusion surrounds my name
Because I don't know why I need you so near
I pray that I am never away from you
I pray that I'll never know that fear

So my name cannot be Drive
Because I cannot only be driven
For all the love you give to me
Cannot be required, it's just a given

So my name cannot be Desire
Because desire is a quest you see
And your love is so much
So much more than a quest to me

So my name cannot be Lustt
Because L-U-S-T-T should mean so much more
It is my **Love, UnderStanding, Tolerance and Trust**
For you who I adore

So I guess my name really is Passion
For my heart is in your constant employ
For within this passion
Is a life of loving and joy

I SAW YOU

I saw you standing

And your beauty blew me away
I admired your sexiness
And you skirts gentle sway

I saw you sitting

With eyes so dark brown and deep
I looked into those eyes for answers
The answers that I seek

I saw you walking

Down the street so very fine
I absorbed your gentle gait
And the curves of your behind

I saw you running

And I hoped it wasn't away
Because in my arms is where I want you
Yes! in my arms to stay

I saw you one day

And had such an urge to meet you
I wish I could get over my shyness
Find the courage just to greet you

I finally met you lady
And I thank God through and through
For giving me the eyes in which

I saw you

THE BLACK WOMAN

In the eyes of a black man
There is no greater vision
Than that of the Black Woman
The only creation in this life
That can capture a man's heart
As she walks progressively towards him
And takes his heart with her
As she walks away
The awe inspiring
Aesthetics of a Black Woman

The penetrating spiritual eyes
The beautiful windows masking the pains endured
The lenses of reflection for the power possessed within

The soulful rich lips
The preceptors of the anticipation of speech
The magnets for desire, touching, kissing
The wondrous body
Formed with the strength to contain powerful passions
Waiting, anticipating, illuminating to be exploded
Upon the truly deserving

Then as control is regained and
Your heart prepares to greet her
She turns to walk away or simply by
And the heart is again captured

For now you see it
You want to
Touch it
Caress it
Possess it
God bless it

Then as simply as the excitement started
It is brought to a crashing end
Until you turn and see another
Black Woman !!!

REALITY

To love me is to know me, Understand me

For as my partner
What I do
Should never come as a shock
But simply as an expected change, an adaptation
My growth

To grow with me is to know me, Trust me

For as my partner
I want and desire for you to grow with me
Change with me, for me, because of me
As I shall for you
Make the beauty we have
Develop into an even greater beauty
Grow into a stronger love
A Love changed yet stronger
Leaving beautiful memories as
We make beautiful occurrences
Appreciating and loving the change

To change with me is to know me, Respect me

For as my partner
We know this is the foundation of our trust
For you nor I will ever do all
That is liked, enjoyed, or admired
For that little flawed habit you didn't mind
In the beginning of our passion
Should not become that annoying identification
That you no longer can tolerate or accept

Because love demands respect
And respect accepts tolerance
And tolerance precedes change

And change is a constant
To our growth

I express these thoughts
To convey one message

My love for you is real
And realness demands reality, and that reality is-

As we met is not how we will stay
We will grow, we will change, we will differ
Yet if we love the reality

We will love

THE TEAR TELLS THE TRUTH

The thought of you just crossed my mind
As I stared out seeing nothing
A tear crept to the corner of my eye
Then rolled out seeking something

Yet, I didn't feel a thing
Not even as it splashed upon my hand
I never noticed the feeling
I just could not understand

I didn't know what love was
Until I felt it wasn't there
I thought I was invincible
Could this tear mean, "I care"?

The thought of being free
Was exciting and oh so fun
Yet, the thought of you not being near
Triggers my tears, they begin to run

Tis true I tell you lady
You have won all parts of my heart
I hope though prayers, faith, and gestures
We will have a brand new start

No words could begin to say
The revelations of that tear
I have found my love in you lady
And it is you that I want to be near

WHY DID I SAY, "I DO?"

This is for me, This is for you
This is a pledge of reality
This is why I said, "I Do"

For I am a black man as is plain to see
Yet you see my darling, you are the world to me

Let me tell you a story
Let's talk about today

Let me express my feelings
Let me tell you why I feel this way

I went out walking today, experiencing the world
and clearing my mind
Then I saw all the beautiful women
and fell in love at least a thousand times

Each one seemed prettier and sexier
than the one seen just before
They caught my eye and made me think
as if life had closed a door

It was then that I arrived at home
after a day of temptation to stray
My feelings were so wound up
that I kneeled and started to pray

Then I spotted you dear
and thoughts of others were left behind
You greeted me with your warm hello
and joy just flooded my mind

Your presence made me feel
such a spectacular good
That I felt I could do anything
and for you I most certainly would

For you I not only hold love
I hold like, respect, and amends
For you are not only my passion
you are my most caring friend

So as humans go
and I'm as human as human can be
I just wanted to tell you lady
how much you and your love mean to me

I have to take the time to tell you
something that you should already know
That through all the temptations, hardships, and grief,
it's you and your love that makes me grow

So if ever there is a time in our life
That I start acting as though we are through
Look me dead in my eye and present this thought
Ask me simply

"WHY DID I SAY I DO?"

DIVORCE

As I lay here so blue and very alone
I've tuned my stereo to the quiet storm

The music plays just on and on, all full of so much love
That the sad songs seem to speak to me like a message from above

I stare out at your picture, which is so straight ahead
Looking at that photograph keeps your face within my head

I play with our pretty puppy as it cuddles up right here
Just wishing, needing, and wanting you to be cuddling with me, my dear

Where did this pain come from and oh so oh why?
I need to recognize this pain yet, I can only sigh

My heart still beats just on and oh so very strong
Yet, without your loving touch it feels so very wrong

Why did we falter with our greatest choice in life?
I was your choice for a man and you my choice for wife

There is a tear that swells inside that no other man should see
Do I really cry for myself or the ending of a special we?

Why didn't it hurt at all when it was all so new?
Guess it was that blinding passion I held down deep for you

And though my thoughts may wonder my love for you was true
Now is the time to realize that we are truly through

This is the one thing in life that I must learn to accept
That our lives together my dear is just a dead subject

The truth for us you see is for us to be apart
Each of us alone again and with a brand new start

THE GOOD DADDY BLUES

I am a good daddy
A strong, good willed, God fearing
child rearing
black man, who definitely is a daddy

Yet, the time, yes, the limited time
I spend with my children is stressed, depressed
and just plain messed - with
By the grip of their mother's long arm of control

I schedule the best
I try hard to impress

I give my caring as a consort
And Damn Right! I pay my child support

Yet, I am eternally bound
As their mother puts and keeps me down

I clearly admit, I made a choice with my life
My children's mother could never be my wife

I have been taken to court
Decided visitation, custody, and support

And though all has been set by law
That woman seeks control of it all

I see it when my children are with me
For my time as their father in life
They are clearly instructed to question me
Thus begins the struggle and strife

My children tell me clearly
Mommy said, "Only she loves me dearly"

They struggle, back talk, and fight
and my responses are met with a
"Mommy said that's not right"

"Mommy's way is the best"
"Daddy we're not impressed"

"Daddy! please where is the phone"
"Mommy said we can come home"

During my guilt and pleading to stay
my children look at me and say
"No thank you daddy. Home is where we want to play"

I tell them that this is their home that I give
They tell me, "Mommy's is where they live"

Then when I decide it's time to fight
All friends and family say, "That's not right"

Don't fight to take the children away
Because it's with their mother that they should stay

So I look to God to show me the way
I harness my anger and start to pray

It was then God touched all parts of my heart
Eased my pain and sent me to their mother to start

So I went to talk and appease
It was then I was dropped to my knees

I had given it all that I had
And she called me a part time DAD!!!

I had tried to do all of this legit
But I was getting sick and tired of this shhhhh-LORD!!

So I returned to my prayers once again
For God was my only friend

And as my heart lay crushed on the ground
The strength of God would not let me stay down

So Heavenly Father I will continue to pray
For the Good Daddy Blues have come my way

I need your blessings as I continue to try
Because without my children

This Good Daddy will surely die

LATE LOVE

Why do we wait to say good-bye before we say I love you?
We wait for the pain of death
Before we realize or pass on the joy of how we really feel

We wait and lay
In anticipatory grief
Before we realize all of the
I'm sorry's
Left unsaid
All the thoughts
Left unexpressed
All the hugs
Left unfulfilled
All the I need you's
Left unspoken

Though we never learn
Even as life after life passes
We become too entwined with ourselves
That we really don't express our caring
Until they are gone
Until they are gone

We wait until the angel of death
Hovers and draws near
To prepare ourselves again
To again be late
Late with our hello's
Late with our good byes

Then because we are again late
The sorrow grows
The pain swells

The tear falls and falls
Now we realize that it's too late to say
I Love You

I KNOW

One Black man raised his voice in prayer
To give thanks for what he knew
Then **GOD** touched his heart and asked,
" SON, WHAT DO YOU KNOW"
The man prayed on and said My Creator

I know
struggle, strife, strain, and sloth
Yet I survive
Because I know

I know
misjudgment, misdeed, mistrust, and mayhem
Yet I survive
Because I know

I know
beatings, blame, blasphemy, and belligerence
Yet I survive
Because I know

I know
crime, cremation, castration, and circumstance
Yet I survive
Because I know

I know
pain, prejudice, persecution, and problems
Yet I survive
Because I know

Through it all I know
You

Then as he passed from the flesh and all that he knew
To the knowing peace of the spirit
He knew

For it was then that the CREATOR
reached out and said

"COME TO ME"
"FOR I KNOW YOU !!!"

LIBATIONS

As our ancestors have faced the truth that is death
And the angel Gabriel has charged Louis, Dizzy, and Miles
To trumpet their swan song
Then, as the sweet soulful music plays,
We remember that not even the Vail of death can stop them
For they shall carry on

For you see they are
The Legends
The Legacies
The stories to be told
They lived their lives with spirit
And at times
Were even a little bold

They are proud that death cannot stop them
For their memories cannot be held at bay
They loved the lives that they touched
Through each and every day

And though the time has come to say goodbye
To the worldly form they keep
In our hearts and in our minds
Their voices will forever speak

They have left us now
And have ventured to GOD'S place
We keep their words, hugs, and expressions and
We will never forget their face

EYES
ON MORE THOUGHTS

I AM ANGRY

Please forgive me my God
For the way I must say it
Please forgive me my people
For the fact that I must say it
But!
I am angry

Angry not only at others
Angry also at my own and myself
Angry for accepting what is offered
Without demanding what is needed, and yes
I am angry

For I have been struggling in this world
As I have traveled far and wide
Whether voluntarily or as a slave
For no other reason than the color of my skin and
The trusting nature of my heart and
I am angry

Angry at the shortcomings of my acceptance
To the responses of my own cries for equality
I have been crying for the nourishment of a meal
Yet, have accepted a biscuit and a glass of water
I ate the biscuit and drank the water
And believed I was full and fulfilled
Though malnutrition was the reality faced,
The biscuit has been digested and the water passed
I am again hungry and
I am angry

I have fought the great battles
And both won and lost
Yet,
Somewhere, sometime, someone put the thought
In my mind that the only battle I am allowed and
Supposed to win is against my own and myself
That terrible thought has divided my people and
I am angry

I have bought into the idea of individualism
Thus causing the development of a me first attitude
Yet, as long as I stand alone
I remain an easy target and am easily shot down
I have been taught the rules, followed the rules and
Found that the rules do not apply to me and
I am angry

I have seen and participated in black on black crime
Well aware that it is self genocide and cancer
Also, well aware that it is the one thing in this life
That only I have the answer
Yet, that thought and that idea allow me
to fail to take the steps needed, and
I am angry

I am angry
At the fates and struggles yet to be faced by my children
Fates and struggles for the same reason as my own
The color of my skin
The trusting nature of my heart
The acceptance of the unreasonable
The self divisiveness
The attempts at an improbable assimilation
The assistance in self genocide
Why did I live at all?

Yet, my greatest anger lies in the belief
That I am powerless to make changes in my life
That it is all right to be angry as long as I am silent
It is time to make changes
It is time to take a stand
It is time to yell to the world

Yes, I am angry!

FEAR

I was born
And
Grew to become a black man
Blessed only with the fear of God
Born in the image of God
The giver of life
The giver of unconditional love
The creator of success

I was born
Then
Why do I fear failure?
For my spirit is the ultimate success
Though failure is all I have ever been labeled
Success is my true reality
For I am success personified

I was born
And
Have dared to dream in the face of injustice
Have dared to die for righteousness
Have dared to fear for the future of my children
Have dared to beautify this world with my presence
Have dared to break the shackles of slavery on my wrist
Yet!
Fear placed them firmly back on my mind
Bright shiny new shackles made of grade "A" fear

I was born
And
Fear that I am not good
Though I am the best
Fear that I am not worthy
Though I am blessed
Fear that I am not one with God
Though in his image I trod

Fear that I am to be judged on my face
Though I am the evidence of God's grace
Fear that I am in control of another
Though I am only in control of this brother
Fear that if I take the lead
I will succeed

I was born
And
Fear even though
I carry, The blood, The genes, The spirit
Of the ancestors to the Creator
Fear even though
I have lived through
Homicide, Genocide, Lack of Pride, Beaten and Tanned Hide

Yet..........
I strive, I thrive, I survive
And though
I am perceived to have fallen
I still lift my praises on high

I was born
And
Have only been taught to rise from failure
So I don't know how to rise from success
Thus I fear success because that would be the end
Of my struggle to survive
Until I remember that success can only be measured
But by one fear

And
I was born
Blessed only with the fear of

God

LABELER

I begin my stance by apologizing
Apologizing
-for being correct
-for being as good as anyone else
-for not being you

For not being a racist---
For I own a pigmentation that identifies me as not of the
Power elite

For not being a sexist---
For sex is a genetic label for the procreation of a species
Not as a means of identification

For not being a fool---
For it is your measure of intelligence and
Not my ability that allows you to label me as such

For being a human---
Identifiable through the genetics and physiology that
establishes
My being

You are---
-the labeler
-the identifier
-the personifier

You have named me through
-color, size, figure, status, class, deeds
Those of my own and others you identify similar to me

Yet, I am only human---
-Susceptible to all
-the same fallacies, and fallibilities
Your whims can conceive

So remember the finger that points away from its owner
Eventually will contract and point at its owner
So as you point, label yourself good
Then label me good as well
For the label you give me
Is the label you will eventually give yourself

PERCEPTION

Perception, deception, inspection, view!
Thus the minute of a black man begins.
The view in the mirror of the self to be expressed
Has yet to be distorted by the view the world
has yet to form.
The view that labels me as a perception of deception
in need of close inspection
To be viewed at all times in all places!

Perception, deception, inspection, pain!
Thus the hour of a black man begins
The pain of the struggles yet to be faced
The struggles of, "no reason," that the world is
preparing to form
The pain of a perception, that I will cause deception,
so maintain the inspection
So the pain will keep me in my place!

Perception, deception, inspection, fear!
Thus the day of a black man begins
The fear of what I may do, can do, and yet haven't done
It's the maybes of the "do's" or of the "done" that the world
braces for
The fear of the perception, the fear of deception, causes over
inspection
The fears that lock me in a place!

Perception, deception, inspection, fantasy!
Thus the year of a black man begins
The fantasy of who I am, what I am, and what I can be
What the world wants to see, but is never prepared for
The fantasy perception, deception, and the justification
for fantasy inspection
The fantasy that locks the mind in the wrong place!

Perception, deception, inspection, truth!
Thus the life of a black man begins
The truth of the view, the pain, the fear, and the fantasy
The truth the world knows, but is hesitant to accept
The truth that if viewed equally, I will rule the minute
The truth that if pain is not present I will progress the hour
The truth that if I'm not feared, I will improve the day
The truth that if the fantasy dies, the years of strength will be revealed!
The truth that in life, I am not
                -----A perception
                    -----Full of deception
                        -----In need of inspection

    I am a black man and I belong in all places!!!!!

PIMP POSITIVE

Well here comes another stereotype shattered!
For I am a *PIMP* and I am positive
So just call me *PIMP POSITIVE*

You see it takes courage to be a positive *PIMP*
Because the acronym has so much negativity associated with it
Yet, I will present how the acronym PIMP should mean more

PIMP in a physical sense to African Americans should mean-
People *In* Much Pain
The pain of loss and struggle
The pain of internal and external genocide
The pain of life itself

PIMP as a thought process to African Americans should mean-
People *In* Many Predicaments
The predicaments of self hate
The predicament of no self love
The predicament of guilt by color

PIMP as an economics indicator to African Americans should mean-
People *Interested* in *Monetary* Progress
The progress of equal and available employment
The progress of social economic equality
The progress of inclusion

PIMP as a military ideology to African Americans should mean-
People *In* Military *Preparation*
The preparation for wars that have no benefit for my people or me
The preparation to return to a segregated racist society once done
The preparation to die at a young age

PIMP as a function of Heritage to African Americans should mean-
People *Inspiring* Many Purposes
The purpose of educating others of our heritage and successes
The purpose of saying no to stereotypes and stigmas
The purpose of telling our children they come from greatness

PIMP as a future outlook to African Americans should mean-
People Intent on Minority oops Majority Progression
The progression that leads to the truth of the lies
The progression that leads to the total destruction of the shackles
The progression that says I am truly free

Just as an acronym such as *PIMP*
Can become *PIMP POSITIVE*
So to can this worlds mind be changed

So I leave my brothers with one final thought
Be a *PIMP*
A **P**erson **I**nterested in **M**y **P**eople again

THAT SIMPLE CLOTH

I have a friend
Yes, a friend who unknowingly awakened my spirit and
Nourished my mind

This friend, a native of a land, long since taken from my
heritage,
Gave me a gift, a simple cloth,
A Shawl
A hand woven, hand-dyed, hand crafted, heritage enriched,
Simple cloth

Yet, that cloth transformed my world
For once it was draped upon my proud black frame
I became a brother to the world
A new world, a confused world,
A world whose spirit has been lost or distorted.

Yes, a brother again recognized
by the Shawl, the garment, an outfit,
A simple cloth
A cloth woven in a land that is the nutrient
Of the very root of my existence.

A simple cloth that in it's visual presence,
Re- invigorated the spiritual bond, the communal nature,
The feeling of oneness amongst us

Yet it was only a cloth, a simple cloth
The man was the same, the job was the same
The goals were the same, the home was the same
The neighborhood was the same, the life was the same
Then how did the self hate change?

How did a simple cloth become a magnet for unity and a
Bulletproof vest against hate and divisiveness?
It's only a simple cloth

Then again, the visual power of that cloth
May serve as a reminder of
The strengths possessed, our heritage, and the spirit of unity
within
The need for remembrance, and repentance
The awakening to wear a simple cloth
Even when we are bare

May the strength of that simple cloth
And all the brotherly love it invoked
Be reflected tomorrow
Even as it hangs in my closet

A BABY CRIES

As a baby cries it's telling us

That it is time to eat
That it is time to sleep
That it is time to change the diaper
That it is time to make it comfortable
That it is time to be held
That it is time to love
A baby is communal and longs for the assistance and closeness of others
This is why a baby cries

Then why when I enter my neighborhood---
Do I see the homeless on the street?
Do I avoid the beggar as if he's plague-infected?
Do I shun the eyes of those I feel will ask me for something?
Do I look unemotionally at an obviously hungry child?
I know why
It's because a baby cries

Then why when I enter my neighborhood---
Do I see the blight upon the working persons faces?
Do I see their quest for relief in the tilt of a bottle or the puff of a weed?
Do I see the stone etchings that are their faces, of the struggles faced and battles fought?
I know why
It's because a baby cries

Then why when I enter my neighborhood---
Do I smell the stench of urine from the unclean streets?
Do I see the young boys fighting and killing each other?
Do I see the hoards of children not going to school?
Do I see parents watch and say it's not my child so why should I care?
Do I see the parents of the uneducated child say he won't listen so why should I care?
I know why
It's because a baby cries

Then why when I enter my neighborhood---
Do I see a child running four blocks out of his way for a safe route home?
Do I see the stress of an innocent six-year-old left to watch their three-year-old sibling?
Do I see a playground strewn with glass and trash?
Do I see a basketball court with no rims and a child with no ball?
Do I see the absence of Mr. Somebody, my neighborhood coach and block captain?
Do I see the absence of Mrs. Somebody, that nosey woman, who always watched me?
Do I see the absence of respect between my parent and my neighbors?
I know why

        It's because a baby cries

Then why when I enter my neighborhood---
Do I see a child pregnant by another child?
Do I see the young girls longing for affection from the young boys?
Do I see the missing fathers not providing the missing hugs?
Do I see the young boys hunting the young girls as if they were prey?
Do I see the missing fathers' lack of guidance and leadership?
Do I see grandmothers anguish over raising two generations of children at the same time?
Do I see a mother's pain for the buried or imprisoned sons?
Do I see the tears for the sons, the babies; she only wants to hold once more?
I know why

        It's because a baby cries

Then why when I enter my neighborhood---
Do I see people giving away their bodies all for the taste of a drug?
Do I see children dressed better than adults?
Do I see children who cannot spell or pronounce the names on the clothes they wear?
Do I see mothers belittling and battling fathers for their lack of support with the children?
Do I see numerous people without suitable, viable, employment or employment at all?
Do I see and sense a feeling of hate---?

---a hate that is territorial within my community
---a hate that says I like you or you are my enemy
---a hate for a person who looks just like you
---a hate, deep hate for oneself

Yet, when another color of face crosses my neighborhood
I sense a different hate and a new sense of respect
---a hate for what that face has done to me and
---a respectful fear that the face can continue to do it to me even
today
Where is the self respect?
Where is the self esteem?
Where is the self awareness?
Where is the self love
I know where and
I know why
          It's because that damn baby continues to cry

My people, My heritage, My culture---
We are but babies in the spiritual context of our life force and we
are crying
We need to look at our heritage, our strength, our pride, our God
and prepare ourselves
We need to move forward with vision, hope, and focus
We need to re-establish our heritage, use the power of our strength
to set a new standard for our pride
We must always remember that we are descendants of a communal
people that could not be killed, and as communal people no one
can move forward without the support and assistance of us all

It is time to feed the baby!
It is time to allow the baby to rest!
It is time to clean the baby out of its waste!
It is time to make the baby comfortable!
It is time to hold the baby!
It is time to love this baby
As no other baby has been loved before!
For a baby abandoned, alone, and crying
Is to suffer a definite fate!

SEEK ME OUT

HEY! BLACK MAN COME HERE AND LET ME TALK WITH YOU!

FOR:

◊   I AM formless, yet my existence is undeniable

◊   I AM powerless yet I make you all powerful

◊   I AM the reason that ignorance is not bliss

◊   I AM the hidden truth in that book you refuse to open

◊   I AM that distorted image in that show you love to watch

◊   I AM the tool you purchase but never use

◊   I AM the reminder of the millions of lineages lost in slavery

◊   I AM the richness of your heritage

◊   I AM the possessor of your self esteem

◊   I AM the beauty of your skin, your soul, your passions

◊   I AM the story woven in the Kinte' cloth you must learn

◊   I AM the message of the talking drums you must respond to

◊   I AM the truth to the unrelenting steam of lies

◊   I AM THE ANSWER GOD GIVES TO YOUR PRAYERS !

FOR I AM KNOWLEDGE

SEEK ME OUT

MAKE ME REAL!!!!!

A BLACK MAN'S EYES

Look into my eyes
A black man's eyes
Look deep if you dare,
and tell me what you see
Tell me all about me

Do you see pain?
A black man's pain
and if you do how
For you're only looking at me,
and pain is a feeling,
and a feeling cannot be seen
only perceived,
and my feelings you could never perceive
Because you are not me

Do you see power?
A black man's power
and if you do how
For you have labeled me powerless
by your actions toward or against my efforts
Yet my power is infinite
So you could not see my power
Because you are not me

Do you see my strength?
A black man's strength
and if you do how
For as my strengths are exposed
you either crush my efforts
or you enslave that strength
in efforts that have no benefit for me nor my people
Do you mistreat and fear my strength
Because you are not me

Do you see my talents ?
A black man's talents
and if you do how
For my ideas are viewed with disfavor
or are stolen and used as your own
or I'm considered for my entertainment worth only
So though I posses many talents
you cannot see them
Because you are not me

Do you see me?
A black man
a person, the human
and if you do how?
For you have not experienced
my struggle,
my heritage,
my strife,
my passions,

You hold no respect for
my pain
my power
my strengths
my talents,
ME

So as you try to use the word empathy
I will use the word empty
Because you are not me
Does the vision seen
deep in this black man's eyes
scare you?

Are you afraid of what you see?
Well you should fear the vision
Because though you are not me
Your actions are what you see reflected
Because I am me

AND I CAN NOW SEE

Printed in the United States
By Bookmasters